MW00886519

What's Your God Language?
Coaching Guide

Dr. Myra Perrine

Copyright © 2011 Dr. Myra Perrine

All rights reserved.

ISBN-13: 978-1467910965
ISBN-10:1467910961

DEDICATION

To Joy O'Byrne,
who cheered me on as I wrote
this Coaching Guide,
and whose commitment to
spiritual formation continually blesses me.

And to Dr. Andree Robinson-Neal
and the leadership of
North Hills Church in San Bernardino, CA,
whose hearts for creating unity and celebration
within their diverse congregation
was an inspiration for this book.

May God richly bless you!

CONTENTS

Introduction

A Framework of Spiritual Formation

ACKNOWLEDGEMENTS

My special thanks to Sharon Leavitt and Tyndale
House Publishers who graciously allowed me to use
the cover of *What's Your God Language?*
and especially to Ruth Berg,
who redesigned this cover;

to my wonderful spiritual companions,
Jeremy Stefano, Dr. Steve Hoke, Ardath Smith,
and all my Imago Christi friends
who've contributed greatly to my understanding of
the inner life with Jesus;

and to Dr. Keith Webb and Tony Stoltzfus for your
continued excellence in coaching.

Thank you!

INTRODUCTION

The Purpose of this Coaching Guide

Welcome to the Coaching Guide for *What's Your God Language?* Perhaps you picked up this book because you are a pastor, small group leader, teacher, or missionary wanting to help others grow in their faith. Or perhaps you are a spiritual director walking along side someone who is learning to identify the fingerprints of God on their lives. Or you may be a parent who's assisting your family to connect with Jesus in authentic ways. Maybe you and your friends are using this book to gain an appreciation for how those around you are 'spiritually wired'.

Whatever your reason, you are about to begin a highly interactive discovery process intended to offer more than information or inspiration. This Coaching Guide was designed to bring *transformation* through providing a venue for reflection, interaction, and support, both in the life of the participant and the coach.[1]

> This Coaching Guide was designed to be used exclusively with the book, *What's Your God Language? Connecting with God Through Your Unique Spiritual Temperament (WYGL?)*.[2] While this guide was not intended to be a primer on coaching, it might be helpful to begin with a short explanation of coaching to serve as an introduction for some or a refresher for others. Because coaching is such an effective growth catalyst, it is recommended that those interested in learning more about it invest in some good resources on the topic.[3]

---

[1] In this Coaching Guide, the person being coached will always be referred to as "the participant."

[2] For the remainder of this Coaching Guide, my book, *What's Your God Language? Connecting with God Through your Unique Spiritual Temperament* (Tyndale, 2007), will be referred to as *WYGL?*

[3] I recommend these coaching books: Tony Stoltzfus, *Leadership Coaching: The Disciplines, Skills, and Heart of a Christian Coach; Christian Life Coaching Handbook: The Calling and Destiny Discovery Tools for Christian Life Coaching; Coaching Questions: A Coach's Guide to Powerful Asking Skills*. I also recommend *TransforMissional Coaching: Empowering Leaders in a Changing Ministry World*, by Steve Ogne and Tim Roehl, and *Coaching 101: Discover the Power of Coaching*, by Dr. Robert Logan & Sherilyn Carlton. In addition, a useful Coaching Skills Seminar is available through Creative Results Management, and Tozer Theological Seminary offers an intensive class called "Leadership Coaching".

An Overview of Coaching

"The purposes of a man's heart are deep waters, but a person of understanding draws them out" (Proverbs 20:5).

What comes to mind when you hear the word *COACH*? Do you picture someone working with an athlete to increase his or her performance?[4] Or do you think of someone who's helping an expectant mother deliver her baby? Well, in this Coaching Guide, when we refer to someone as a coach, we are speaking about a person who *listens and asks focused questions to help another move forward in life.*

You may be thinking you're already a pretty good listener, and if so, you could be off to a good start. Coaching in this book, however, involves a particular kind of listening: it's *listening with the intention of moving someone forward.* And though some of us might listen pretty well, most of us do not have the type of *listening and asking* skills we need to be an effective coach, because if we're honest with ourselves, it's really easier to *talk and tell* than it is to *ask and listen.* Yes, we all have a great deal to learn when it comes to focusing on what another person is saying—being 100% present to them—for more than a few minutes at a time… before switching the conversation back to us. Try it sometime by

---

[4] For ease in reading, this guide will now alternate using "his" or "her" to represent both genders.

5

attempting to listen to a person for 15 minutes as he talks, and without redirecting the conversation back to you, keep his discovery process going by using some of the following phrases:

- Is that so?
- Tell me more.
- How did that make you feel?
- This seems quite important to you.
- Really?
- You did, huh?
- Then what?
- I see.
- Wow!
- You don't say.
- That is really something!
- Hmmm.
- No kidding.
- How about that.
- Interesting.[5]

Fully attending to someone else is not as easy as it sounds, is it? Being able listen well is a skill, and skills always take time and effort to learn.

An effective coach is not only a good listener; she also knows her way around helpful questions. Unlike a mentor who *dispenses expertise* **to** *others*, a coach is one who *distills awareness* **from** *others*. While a mentor guides people from his own experience by using the wisdom he's gained along the way, a coach is a

---

[5] This list was adapted from Dann Farrlley's "Brave Communication" DVD at ibethel.com.

catalyst for self-discovery. There is indeed an important place for both coaches and mentors; however, this guide is primarily designed to help those who are coaching others through the book *WYGL?* provide a safe environment where the emphasis is more on *listening and asking* than on *fixing or advising*… as the coach endeavors to find out where the participant wants to go and grow, and then assists her in getting there.

Important Distinctions in Helping Roles

It may be useful to define different helping roles so people know what it means to be a coach—and what it does not!

A Coach is a person who helps another move ahead in life by listening, then asking insightful questions to draw out answers, wants, needs, ideas, motivations, and reflections—unearthing deep beliefs that lie within the other. Coaches are forward thinking, helping individuals or groups move toward their own goals. Coaches foster a safe place for dialogue so that others can make their own discoveries, gain personal insights, and create their own action steps. Not teachers per se, coaches are skilled, encouraging companions who provide support and clarification as progress takes place.

A Therapist is someone who seeks to discover unhealthy issues or problems a client may be having by looking at the past and helping him deal with roots that are now blocking his forward movement. (For the purposes of this Coaching Guide, if you are helping someone who is suffering from depression, marriage or family problems, addictions, etc., it is wise to refer him to a professional counselor).

A Mentor is a person with expertise in a particular area who uses that knowledge to shape the individualized learning of a psychologically healthy person. Mentors provide knowledge, advice, guidance, and correction mostly in areas where they have expertise, usually within their own domain or profession.

A Pastoral Counselor is a trained professional who listens with God's caring heart and mind to someone who may be in pain or facing an important decision, then offers suggestions and prayer that allows God's truth and grace to bring change, comfort, and consolation to that person.

A Spiritual Director is someone who aids others in seeing, hearing, or sensing the presence and movement of God's Spirit in her life, helping her deal with issues that may be keeping her 'stuck', then providing assistance to navigate the changing spiritual seasons of her journey with God.[6]

---

[6] This list was created and revised by Keith Webb and Myra Perrine.

A Theology of Coaching

"But the Counselor, the Holy Spirit, whom the Father will send in My name, will teach you all things and will remind you of everything I have said to you" (John 14:26).

Jesus has given an amazing Gift to His followers: His own Spirit! The indwelling Holy Spirit is our Counselor and the One who teaches and imparts wisdom to His children as we depend upon Him (John 14:15-18, 26; Eph 1:17; 1Cor 2:11; James 1:5, 3:15-18). Christian coaches must lean heavily upon the Holy Spirit in their coaching dialogues, and though their experience and discernment may inform their questions, they are aware that only God can give them the capacity to be an effective coach. Thus, it is vital for the person using this Coaching Guide to pray often—before, after, and during each coaching session—in order to discern the voice and leading of the Holy Spirit.[7]

While the Lord has given us His own Spirit to help us grow and mature, He has also given us His people—the Body of Christ (I Cor. 12, Eph. 4). Therefore in coaching, spiritual discernment is often a "body" concept: one person in the body comes

---

[7] God's people hear God's voice in various ways. For a good resource in learning to discern what God is saying, I recommend Brad Jersak's book, *Can You Hear Me? Tuning In to the God Who Speaks* (Monarch Books, 2006).

alongside another to ask compelling questions that bring God's truth to light.[8] Thus, a Christian coach's primary job is to open a path to the inward movement of the Holy Spirit in the participant's life; this is done by inviting him to reflect as the Spirit is leading him in that moment, which makes coaching a practical tool for personal transformation.

Because this guide was designed to facilitate spiritual growth in both the coach and the participant alike, a FRAMEWORK of SPIRITUAL FORMATION has been added in the back of this book. It provides a biblical model for growing into the likeness of Christ, and also offers additional reflection and coaching questions that can be used at each stage of a believer's spiritual development.[9]

---

[8] Interestingly, the word *persona* in Latin comes from the Greek word *prosopon*, which means "face to face."

[9] The reflection and coaching questions at the back of this book were developed from 1 John 2:12-14.

Integrating Two Coaching Models

To enable Coaches to assist participants as they journey through *WYGL?*, this guide integrates two coaching models: *The Coaching Conversation* and *The COACH Model.*

The Coaching Conversation[10]

In the first model, there are four simple steps that guide a coach through the conversation:

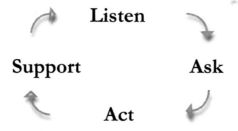

Listen

Ask

Act

Support

LISTEN: The coach focuses her attention on what the participant is saying.

ASK: The coach moves the conversation forward by using questions that prompt the participant to explore more deeply and discover new insights.

---

[10] This model is adapted from *Leadership Coaching*, by Tony Stoltzfus (BookSurge Publishing, 2005).

ACT: The coach helps the participant find a focus, think through options, choose the best solution, and set concrete action steps.

SUPPORT: The coach and participant celebrate wins together as the coach affirms choices and provides accountability.

The COACH Model:
Connect, Outcome, Awareness, Course, Highlights[11]

Another helpful model is the Coach Model, which incorporates five steps: Connecting, Outcome, Awareness, Course, and Highlights (i.e., COACH). Each of these steps moves the participant through the coaching session.

Copyright © 2004 Keith E. Webb

---

[11] The COACH Model™ © 2004 Keith E. Webb. Used with permission. www.activeresults.com.

CONNECT: *Engaging the participant*
The first thing a coach does when using this model is
to spend a few moments building rapport with the
participant at the beginning of each meeting. The
relationship between the coach and participant helps
foster a trusting spiritual link between the Holy
Spirit, the coach, and the participant, and the ***bond of
trust and safety*** is the key in the CONNECT phase.
Some questions you might ask while connecting are:

- How have you been?
- What's been happening in your life?
- What's the Lord been showing you or doing
  since we last met?

OUTCOME: *Determining where the participant wants
to go*
In this phase, the coach asks what the participant
would like to accomplish during his time with you
that day. While the coach guides the dialogue,
together the duo determines how to best use their
time together. This usually means following up on
previous topics, then engaging in new ones.
Establishing ***direction*** is the key in the OUTCOME
phase. Here are a few questions to use:

- What would you like to take away from
  our time together today?
- What do you want to discuss specifically as
  a follow up to our last appointment?
- What would make today's conversation
  successful for you?

AWARENESS: *Stimulating reflective dialogue*
Here the coach asks powerful questions, then
practices active listening—listening beyond the
participant's words. By encouraging insight through
a reflective dialogue, the coach also gives feedback
by mirroring back what she's heard, then getting
confirmation and clarity from the participant. *Self-
discovery* for the participant is the key in the
AWARENESS phase. Some questions might be:
> • What are you learning in this process?
> • What might be some of the keys to
> understanding what's happening here?
> • What do you think the Lord may be saying
> to you through this?
> • What other factors might be influencing
> your decision?
> • How might you move forward?

COURSE: *Crafting specific action steps*
This phase seeks to capture the insights gained
during your time together and put them into a
'what's next' plan. Here the coach and participant
continue their reflective dialogue, but now they focus
on a future course of action. The result will be clear
steps the participant designs and commits to do
before the next coaching conversation. Establishing
two or three action steps for each topic is ideal, since
action items are the key to the COURSE phase. Some
questions you might use are:
> • What actions would you like to take this
> week?

• How often and when will you do these?
• Since an inch is a synch and a yard is too hard, how can we break down that plan into bite-sized pieces?
• On a scale of 1-10 (10 being high), how confident are you that you can accomplish this plan? (If 7 or below, it might be good to go back and rework the plan.)
• What obstacles do you anticipate facing?
• What are some tools you might use to overcome those obstacles?

HIGHLIGHTS: *Remembering, synthesizing, and voicing learning and valuable take-aways*
At the end of each session, it is helpful to ask the participant to restate his insights and 'ah ha's' from the session, anything gained he is now taking with him in the way of new learning, awareness, or helpful ideas. This review empowers the participant to deepen his learning, and it also helps the coach know what the participant found most valuable. *Synthesized learning* is the key in the HIGHLIGHTS phase. This is also a good time to ask the participant to repeat his action steps. Sample questions are:
• What parts of our discussion today were most significant for you?
• What would you like to remember from our time that was particularly helpful?
• What are your biggest take-aways?
• What awareness or 'ah ha's' do you now have that you didn't before?

Additional Coaching Tips

In this Coaching Guide, these two models have been integrated into a simple, blended process. In addition, you might find the following tips helpful as you begin to coach:

1. The most important element in coaching is the relationship you, the coach, have with the participant. Therefore, as you begin, you may find you'll need to adjust some of the weekly sessions to meet your dual needs. For example, the lessons in this guide were written for a 60 to 90 minute meeting every other week, but you might decide the two of you require a longer time together, or you may want to take an extra week to cover a lesson because the participant needs more time discussing that content. *Always feel free to adapt this material to your particular situation.* Moving the process forward while attending to your coach-participant needs is the key to maximizing your experience.

2. Each coaching lesson contains a large number of questions from which you, the coach, must choose. *Please select only those questions that are appropriate and helpful to your participant*—taking into consideration the amount of time you have for each appointment. The goal is not to discuss all the

questions, but to assist the participant as he grows in his love for God. As long as that is happening, the process is working, even if the majority of questions have not been addressed.

3.   Because the questions in this Coaching Guide were created to stimulate serious thought and discussion, it's essential to *pause* after each one and be prepared to *wait* for a thoughtful response. **Expect silence.** If the participant says, "I don't know," that is more than okay—it is a good sign that she is going beyond a surface reply. While you may need to ask her a clarifying question, it's important to give her all the time she needs to think through her answers, as well as permission to take her 'best guess'—even though she may want to retract or amend later her statements later. Coaching is about 'thinking out-loud' together, and the nature of the process includes being willing to risk. Thus, the more comfortable you are with predictable silences and spontaneous answers, the more material will be available for the participant to chew on during the week.

4.   There will undoubtedly be times when you'll need to formulate your own coaching questions. A good principle for constructing questions is to *make them as open-ended as possible (versus asking a YES/NO question or*

one that can be answered with one word).
This can be done by beginning your question
with, **"WHAT"** or **"HOW"**. For example, you
may be talking about the participant's prayer
life. By simply starting the sentence with,
"WHAT" or "HOW" (versus "why", which
can imply judgment), you might ask:

- "What are you currently enjoying
  about your prayer life?" or
- "What does talking to God look like
  for you?"
- "How might your conversations
  with God become more meaningful in
  your relationship with Him?"
- "What next steps could you take to
  see your prayer life become more like
  the one you desire it to be?"

Thus, formulating open-ended questions will
generate more self-discovery and growth.

5. When creating your own questions, it is also
   important to *avoid "leading questions" that
   guide the participant to your assumed
   answer.* For example, instead of saying,
   "How could you have a better prayer life?"
   (which assumes several things that might not
   be true!), you might ask, "If you could have
   the conversational relationship with God you
   wanted—one that would make you both
   happy—how might that look?" The more
   your questions don't imply there is a right
   and wrong answer, the more safety, self-

discovery, exploration, and reflection will be generated—all ingredients essential for growth.

6. When coaching others, it is also good to *write down all the Action Steps the participant verbalizes during your time together,* encouraging her to write them down as well. Since these statements become commitments of what the participant will do between sessions, having them written down makes the items more concrete, helps you revisit them during your next appointment, and also sends the message that you'll be checking back the next time you're together to see what she has done with her desired steps.

7. Before you begin coaching through *WYGL?,* be sure you have *read and familiarized yourself with the entire book.* That will make it easier for you to avoid answering questions that *WYGL?* will address in later chapters. It's also beneficial to be thoroughly familiar with this Coaching Guide and the lesson you will cover before you meet with the participant, highlighting those questions you are hoping to discuss.

8. If several people in your faith community are simultaneously coaching people through *WYGL?,* you may want to *meet together on a regular basis to offer each other support—*

even practicing asking questions with one another—especially if you are new to coaching. Getting together with others provides ongoing encouragement, and will also give you a place to ask any questions that may arise as you proceed.

9. While the coach-participant relationship is very important, if you begin to sense that the participant is not coming to your sessions prepared—having consistently not read the up-and-coming chapter in *WYGL?* or completed his action items—you may want to *discuss whether this is the best time for him to complete this study*, given his prior commitments, life-circumstances, whatever. Though it's a difficult judgment call, you may have to decide together that these coaching sessions need to be put on 'hold' for awhile, rescheduled, or ended altogether if the participant is not in a place where continued meeting is beneficial.

10. In conclusion, it's always good to keep in mind that the coaching process is for the participant, with the focus of your time being on her relationship with the Lord; you are simply serving as the facilitator. However, as you build trust, it may be important for you to share from your own life, because *mutual self-disclosure can strengthen the coach-participant bond.* But as the coach, guard

against allowing 'your story' to become the center of the conversation, keeping in mind that you are sharing *primarily* for the purpose of supporting the participant's journey.

Once you're familiar with the two coaching models and these suggested tips, you are ready to start using this Coaching Guide. Now ... let the adventure begin!

1

~ Coaching Session One ~
Getting Acquainted

Outcomes:
1. To establish an environment of trust & safety with the participant;
2. To share your faith journey and hear the participant's story;
3. To determine if the participant would like to commit to eight coaching sessions that focus on deepening his relationship with God;
4. To introduce the book, *WYGL?*
5. To invite the participant to read the Preface and Introduction of *WYGL?* before you meet again.

CONNECT
• Greet the participant and find out how life is going in general. Put him at ease by listening as he shares about his life.

AWARENESS/ASK/LISTEN
• Talk a bit about the purpose of this meeting. Explain how you (and perhaps others from your church, youth group, office, school, Bible Study, whatever) are beginning to explore ways to grow in your love relationship with Jesus by utilizing the book, *WYGL?*

• Share how you will also be using a process called 'coaching' to walk with others through *WYGL?* and describe how coaching is different from mentoring or spiritual direction (though there may be some overlap), because coaching primarily involves more listening, reflection, self-discovery, and discussion.
> • Explain that this first meeting is to help you get to know one another better.
> • Allow time for questions along the way.

• Share briefly how you came to know the Lord, including what is motivating you to want to deepen your relationship with God in this season of life.

• Ask about the participant's relationship with Jesus, and invite him to share a bit of his faith-journey as you use some of the following questions:

• Tell me how you came to know the Lord.[12]
• What circumstances inspired you to give your life to Jesus?
• What were you hoping would happen in your life when you trusted Christ?
• What were you expecting your spiritual life to look like by this time?
• In what ways has your life changed since you met Jesus? In what ways do you still want your life to change?
• If you could describe the overall satisfaction you are experiencing now in your relationship with God by giving it a number between 1 to 10 (10 being "very satisfied" and 1 being "very dissatisfied"), what number would you choose? Share why you selected that number.
• If you could draw a picture of what you'd like your relationship with Jesus to look like by this time next year, describe your picture of how it would look.
• How might your desires for spiritual growth be enhanced by journeying with others over the next few months?

ACTION
• Tell him you would be honored if he would join you (and possibly others in your faith community) as

---

[12]Occasionally you may find yourself talking to someone who has never committed his life to Jesus. This becomes an exciting opportunity to lead that person to Christ and explore his desire to know God personally.

you grow in your passion for God.

> • Ask if he has the time and desire to commit to
> eight sessions over the next few months. If he so,
> continue through this coaching session. If he is
> not interested or doesn't have time at this point
> in his life, let him know that this opportunity
> will be available to him at a later date.

• If he chooses to continue, introduce him to the
book, *WYGL?* and be sure he has his own copy. Share
with him that you (and your church, youth group,
office, school, etc.), will be working through this
book together, not only to grow individually, but
also as a faith community.

• Explain how the coaching sessions will begin by
him reading the Preface through the Introduction
(from the beginning of the book though page 3) of
WYGL?

> • Ask him to highlight what is meaningful to
> him.

• Discuss your hope that your relationship will be a
safe one, a place where both of you can be honest
and authentic with one another during the time
together. Assure him of your commitment to keep
your conversations confidential.

• Because we get more when we invest more, invite
him to do the exercises in the Introduction.

• Set a time to meet, preferably in one to three weeks.

• Ask him if there are other ways he would like to commit to growing in his relationship with God this week (such as scheduling more time for prayer or taking a walk with God, reading his Bible more often, listening to worship music, attending church, sitting in silent medication, exploring Christian art, taking a whole day of rest on the Sabbath, etc.). Find out if he'd like you to keep him accountable by asking how he's doing with these commitments the next time you meet.

• Don't forget to write down any Action Steps the participant verbalizes, and encourage him to write them down as well so the two of you can revisit them when you meet again.

SUPPORT/HIGHLIGHTS
• In closing, share what you've enjoyed most about your time together today, and ask the participant if there have been any highlights for him, anything that was particularly important or helpful?

• Ask what he is most looking forward to in working through *WYGL?* together.

• Encourage him in his desire and decision to grow in his relationship with the Lord.

• Close in prayer.

• [After the appointment ends, reflect on your coaching session; then fill in the following journal page that will help you grow in your skills as a coach.]

~ Taking Time to Reflect on Today's COACHING Session ~

(SEE SAMPLE JOURNAL ENTRY ON NEXT PAGE)

Participant's name:_____ Date:_____

During the appointment, what was happening in you while you were coaching? _____
_____
_____
_____
_____

What did you learn about yourself today as you were coaching? _____
_____
_____
_____
_____

What did you learn from today's appointment about this participant? _____
_____
_____
_____
_____

What would you like to do differently next time? Any prayer items? _____
_____
_____
_____

~ SAMPLE ~
~ Taking Time to Reflect on Today's COACHING Session ~

Participant's name: _Chris Jones_ Date: _Oct 25ᵗʰ_

•During the appointment, what was happening in you while you were coaching? _I felt a bit nervous and realized it would have helped if I'd have re-read and studied the Coaching Guide more thoroughly before our appointment._

•What did you learn about yourself today as you were coaching? _I learned I really enjoy coaching, but at times, I tend to jump to conclusions before asking enough questions. I also realzed I feel a bit awkward talking about my own relationship with God, but I know I will grow through this process._

•What did you learn from today's appointment about this participant? _Chris likes to talk! Sometimes the conversation went off tract because I didn't' redirect it back to the topic at hand._

•What would you like to do differently next time? Any prayer items? _I want to reread the coaching chapter and make more notes beforehand, as well as highlighting the questions I want to ask so our conversation flows more naturally. I also want to pray daily for Chris, & pray more before we meet again._

2

~ Coaching Session Two~
Beginning the Process of Spiritual Reflection

Outcomes:
1. To continue building a relationship of safety and trust with the participant;
2. To discuss the Forward and Introduction in *WYGL?* and help the participant reflect more on her relationship with God— especially in light of God's "Great Invitation";
3. To help her identify her current desire to go deeper with God;
4. To introduce Chapter 1 in *WYGL?*

CONNECT
• Greet the participant and find out about her week.

• Continue building rapport, safety and trust.

• Find out how things have been in her relationship with God since you were last together (through any areas where she invited accountability the last time you met). Ask how she's doing with any Action Items you both wrote down.

• Review how you desire that your relationship will be a safe place where both of you can be honest and authentic. Remind her of your commitment to keep your conversations confidential.

• Ask if she read the Forward and Introduction in *WYGL?* What does she think of the book so far?

AWARENESS/ASK/LISTEN
• The Introduction of *WYGL?* talks about God's "invitation and longings." Ask the participant:
> • What do you feel about the Lord being a "longing God" (page xiv)—One who *desires* for a relationship with *you?*
> • In what ways do you sense the Lord drawing you to Himself, reminding you of His love?
> • On a scale from 1-10 (10 being high) how much do you experience God's desire for you?
> • Describe your own desire for greater closeness or intimacy with Jesus. What number

between 1-10 (10 being high) would you give your own spiritual hunger?
> • What do you think is contributing to that hunger?
> • What might cause your hunger to increase or decrease?

• In *WYGL?* some people described themselves as spiritually frustrated, dry, stuck, or confused. Ask the participant to circle the words that best describe how she is experiencing God during this season; share the words *you* checked off as well—those words that best describe *your* relationship with God right now—and after she shares her words, you share yours:

Stuck	Fun	Stale
Fresh	Alive	Boring
Deeply satisfying	Frustrating	Confusing
Spirit-led	Dry	Mysterious
Up & down	Wonderful	Scary
Guilt-producing	Intimate	Aloof
Guilt-free	Difficult	Comforting
Meaningful	Routine	Close
Service-driven	Joyous	Revelatory
A fight to do right	Light & easy	Trusting
Word-centered	Adventurous	Distant
Same old, same old	Battle-weary	Open
Hungry for more	Obedience-driven	Uncertain

• Discuss how you both feel as you look at the words you chose.

• Invite her to describe a time in her life when she

felt very close to God?

> • What were the circumstances, or what was happening around her during that time?
> • Looking back, what does she think caused her to experience that closeness with God?

• In the Preface of *WYGL?* on page x, the book talks about how our way of relating to God can grow and change as we walk with Him over time, i.e., it often broadens and deepens. Ask:

> • How have you seen your relationship with God broaden, deepen, or grow during the time you've known Him?
> • What do you think has contributed to those changes?

• On page xiv of *WYGL?* the author speaks of all humanity being "homesick" for our initial garden life with God, the one Adam and Eve had, i.e., the closeness and face-to-face access they had to God before the fall as they walked and talked together, enjoying the meaningful work He'd given them, experiencing the animals, beauty, colorful flowers, and all the food they could eat in a perfect world with ideal health (without pain or aging)… all while the ground was being watered by surrounding rivers and a constant mist!

> • Discuss times you've experienced this 'homesickness' for that initial garden life with God, longing for God's goodness, beauty, love, and joy.

• Talk about ways each of you 'lose touch' with your longing for 'home. What keeps you so busy you can't feel that desire for the abundant, rich life God's designed you to enjoy with Him?

• On page xi and xii of *WYGL?*, Henri Nouwen says: *"until we are in touch with our own belovedness, we cannot touch the sacredness of another; until we embrace whom God has made us to be, we will continually try to make others over in our own likeness and image."*
  • Discuss the importance of knowing our own 'belovedness'—how deeply *wanted* we are by God, and how knowing that allows us to love and celebrate others to the fullest.
  • Have a conversation about ways we tend to try and 'fix' or 'change' people who might not answer the questions in this Coaching Guide like we would—even though they love God.

• There is a parable in the Introduction of *WYGL?* on page xv about God looking into a mirror and seeing His own image, then breaking the mirror into a million pieces—each piece becoming a human soul, and each soul bringing something of the image of God to the world.
  • As God's image bearer, what aspect of God's image do you bring to the world, i.e., His order, beauty, creativity, analysis, fun, etc.?
  • How do you think God's image in you keeps you longing for communion with Him, your Creator?

• Page xv of *WYGL?* explains that the Celts believed in *thin places*—spaces, places, and moments where the unseen and the seen momentarily collide, allowing the veil separating the eternal from the temporal to become so thin and permeable that—through a vibrant sunset or a child at play—one could almost breathe celestial air, so to speak. Ask the participant:

> • Consider some of your *thin places*, those times and places where you most often hear the gentle invitation of Jesus to dwell with Him. Where and when do those *thin places* usually happen for you?
>
> • At the end of the Introduction, the author uses a dance metaphor to characterize our life with Jesus, describing how *the dance* can take on two distinctly different forms:
>
> > *"When we were first invited to dance [with the Lord], many of us began with a simple response... [and life was] easier when we fixed our eyes on our Partner's face and relaxed into Him as our strong Leader ....*
> >
> > *"In this dance, there are points of exhilaration and joy like we've never known before, yet we don't really need to know what's ahead because our Partner knows and He is leading. All we need to do is stay engaged in the dance and keep our eyes on Him in full surrender.*
> >
> > *"Of course, there is another way we can respond ... not fully engaged with Jesus at all, spending most of our time looking*

*around at what others are doing, learning
the 'right' steps, trying to look cool, and
now and then glancing at our partner with a
nod.... A dance like this isn't a tandem act;
it's more of a solo performance. And this
dance, of course, gets old. We find that we
are constantly working to improve our style
and do the steps better. But deep inside, we
know this isn't the abundant dance Jesus
invited us to. He wants us to be fully
present to Him as He is fully present to
us—leading, guiding, moving us across the
floor with exhilaration. His dance is new
every morning, for in our Partner's presence
there is fullness of joy (Psalms 16:11)."*

• Discuss how the participant's life is like a *dance*
with the Lord by asking:

> • What does your 'dance' with Jesus look
> like, and who is leading your dance—you or
> Jesus?
> • In what ways have you gotten caught up in
> what other dancers are doing or what they
> may be thinking about you?
> • Are you concentrating more on doing the
> steps correctly than enjoying your partner's
> company and embrace?
> • In what ways have you walked off the floor
> or even tried changing partners?
> • Would you characterize your dance as an
> independent cha cha, an exuberant swing
> dance, or an intimate waltz?

• How are you learning new steps with Him?
• What would you like your dance to be like if you could redesign it today?
• Is there anything keeping you from 'going for it' in your dance with the Lord?

ACTION
• In light of all that you have discussed, ask how the participant would like to take action this week to move more intentionally toward the God who is: *"always beckoning us to Himself, always pressing in, longing for connection, even disturbing us with His consistent, irrepressible love"*? Suggest she write down the steps she'd like to take this week.

• Share how *WYGL?* is going to name and describe nine unique ways each of us connects with God. Ask her to read Chapter 1 about the spiritual temperaments before you meet next time, and have her highlight things that are most meaningful to her in the chapter.

• Don't forget to write down any Action Steps the participant verbalizes, and encourage her to write them down as well so you can revisit these commitments the next time you are together.

• Invite her to do the exercises in Chapter 1 of *WYGL?* (pgs 5, 9, 10, 15).

• Set a time to meet again in one to three weeks.

SUPPORT/HIGHLIGHTS

• In closing, share what you've enjoyed most about your time together today, and ask if there have been any helpful insights for her, any parts of the discussion that were particularly important?

• Encourage her in any ways you can from your conversation today.

• Both close in conversational prayer.

• [After the appointment, reflect on your coaching session and fill in the following journal page to help you grow in your skills as a coach.]

~ Taking Time to Reflect on Today's COACHING Session ~

Participant's name:_____ Date:_____

During the appointment, what was happening in you while you were coaching? _____
_____
_____
_____
_____

What did you learn about yourself today as you were coaching? _____
_____
_____
_____

What did you learn from today's appointment about this participant? _____
_____
_____
_____

What would you like to do differently next time? Any prayer items? _____
_____
_____
_____

3

~ Coaching Session Three ~
Understanding the Spiritual Temperaments

Outcomes:
1. To continue building a relationship of trust with the participant;
2. To discuss the concept of Spiritual Temperaments found in Chapter 1, and how his Spiritual Temperaments effect his relationship with God;
3. To introduce Chapter 2-3 in *WYGL?* including the Spiritual Temperament Inventory.

CONNECT
• Greet the participant and find out what's been going on since you last met. Ask how he's been doing with any Action Items you both wrote down.

• Find out what the participant liked best about Chapter 1 of *WYGL?* Field any questions.[13]

AWARENESS/ASK/LISTEN
• Talk for a few moments about some of his favorite things: food, sports, vacation spots, etc.
> • How does he feel about enjoying things for which others may not have a liking?
> • How might this same thing relate to selecting a church, a worship style, even a way of loving and serving God?

• Discuss what it means for him to be 'connected with God'.
> • Look up John 15:4-5, or read it from *The Message*: *"Live in Me. Make your home in Me just as I do in you. In the same way that a branch can't bear grapes by itself but only by being joined to the vine, you can't bear fruit unless you are joined with Me. I am the Vine, you are the branches. When you're joined with Me and I with you, the relation intimate and organic, the harvest is sure to be abundant.*

---

[13] Be sure to allow his questions to be an incentive for continuing the journey through *WYGL?*, and try not to answer any questions that will be discussed later in the book.

Separated, you can't produce a thing" (John 15:4-5, *The Message).*
  • What do you think Jesus meant when He talked about: 'Living in Him, making our home in Him, remaining joined with Him intimately and organically?'
  • Discuss what that connection with God looks like for him.

• Talk about the story in Chapter 1 of *WYGL?* involving Beth, who had accepted a generic "one-size-fits all" formula for spiritual growth, and how she needed encouragement to meet God in ways that were authentic and real for her (since her preferences didn't line up with how others around her were connecting with God). Ask the participant:
  • Are there ways that you might have accepted a "one-size-fits-all" formula for spiritual growth, and what does that formula look like for you?
  • If you were going to try to imitate or copy someone's relationship with God, whose relationship would you choose and why?
  • How has that person been helpful to you in your spiritual life?
  • How might it be counter-productive to copy that person's way of loving and serving God?

• Share with the participant how and when you first learned about your own spiritual temperament, and talk about the ways your journey has changed since you realized how you are 'uniquely wired', i.e., how you best and most naturally connect with God.

43

• Ask the participant to reflect back on his life—the remarkable times he's had in his journey with the Lord. What experiences brought him the most joy and closeness, such as:

> • Powerful times of worship?
> • Special moments with God in solitude and silence?
> • Important moments in scripture?
> • Being around beauty in a sacred place?
> • Meaningful acts of service for Jesus?
> • Being outdoors… at the beach or in the mountains?
> • Watching children play in unselfconscious enthusiasm?

• Give the participant plenty of time to describe some of the most precious and significant encounters he's had with the Lord.

• Help him identify the most genuine and meaningful ways he connects with God—the *how, when, and where* of his 'sacred space'.

• Affirm him in these.

• *WYGL?* describes nine categories or pathways that stir our passion for God—ways we feel inspired, filled, held, or provoked in our love for God.[14]Ask which of these nine spiritual temperaments the participant indentifies with most:

---

[14] These nine Spiritual Temperaments are taken from Gary Thomas' book, *Sacred Pathways* (Zondervan, 2002).

• The Activist—loving God through confrontation with evil?
• The Ascetic—loving God through solitude and simplicity?
• The Caregiver—loving God through serving others?
• The Contemplative—loving God through adoration?
• The Enthusiast—loving God through mystery and celebration?
• The Intellectual—loving God through the mind?
• The Naturalist—loving God through experiencing Him out-of-doors?
• The Sensate—loving God through the senses?
• The Traditionalist—loving God through ritual and symbol?

• With which temperaments does he identify least?

• The book describes spiritual temperaments in several ways. Ask the participant which of these explanations he personally likes best by finishing this sentence: "For me a, Spiritual Temperament is…"
_____My best and most natural way of relating to God.
_____A genre God uses to tell me His story.
_____My 'entry point' into greater awareness of God's presence.
_____Where I find my 'sacred space' with the Lord.
_____The most meaningful way I love Jesus.
_____The place my spiritual passion is stirred.
_____How, where, and what quiets me inside.

_____A clue directing my thoughts heavenward.

_____That which inspires hunger for unseen realities.

_____Not a tidy box that explains everything about
me and my life with God.

_____What brings life and spiritual refreshment to me.

_____Involuntary ways I am drawn to God and find
myself thinking about Him.

_____God's gift to me, my gift back to Him, my gift to
the Body of Christ and the world.

_____A way to help me understand others and give
them grace and acceptance.

_____One more piece of the puzzle of how God has
'uniquely wired' me.

_____Not a label I can use to totally describe myself or
someone else.

_____A God-shaped spiritual preference that, though
my environment may have influenced it, was
given to me by God.

• To help the participant understand spiritual
temperaments better, discuss how they can be
expressed by similes—figures of speech that
compare differing things by using the word *'like'* or
'as'. For example, one might say:
"A Spiritual Temperament is *LIKE*…"
  • The start-up system on my computer **because**
    God hard-wired it into me;
  • A nap in the afternoon **because** it revives me;
  • A God-commercial for something yummy to
    eat **because** when I see it, my hunger for God is
    enlivened, and it's difficult for me to ignore the
    Lord.

• Now ask the participant to try writing a simile of his own to describe what a spiritual temperament is *LIKE* to *him*: "A Spiritual Temperament is *LIKE*…"

• _____*because*

_____.

• _____*because*

_____.

• Here are some other similes people have written: "A Spiritual Temperament is *LIKE*…"
  • A kayak *because* it parts the waters as I travel through life;
  • Chocolate *because* it satisfies my craving for God;
  • A walk in the brook *because* as the water rushes over me, I feel cleansed and refreshed;
  • A pair of spiritual glasses *because* it helps me see God more clearly;
  • A musical instrument *because* when united with others, I become part of God's symphony.

• Be sure the participant truly understands what a spiritual temperament is before you move on, i.e., a God-given preference in the spiritual realm that becomes the most fundamental and natural way of knowing and loving God.
  • If he is struggling with understanding this, return to the lists in this section.

• Discuss any other thoughts the participant has about how he or others best connect with God.

ACTION
• Find out in what ways the participant would like to continue pursuing God and growing in his new understanding of his 'spiritual wiring' this week.

• Offer the following suggestions:
  • Interview a few people this week for 10 or 15 minutes, and ask how each one best connects with God and experiences closeness with Him.
  • Then note how their responses are similar or different than yours.
  • Pay attention to what you are doing and where you are when you sense your desire for God being stirred. Record your impressions this week.

• Read Chapters 2 and 3 this next week and do the exercises on pages 34, 35, 36, 47, 52, 57, 63, 67, 73, 79, 86, 94-95.

• It's important to have the participant take the Spiritual Temperament and Spiritual Practice Inventories in Chapter 2 (pages 21-34) before you next meet, and bring the results from those Inventories with him to your next meeting.

• Write down any Action Items the participant verbalizes, and encourage him to write them down as well so you can revisit these commitments the next time you are together.

SUPPORT/ HIGHLIGHTS

• In closing, share what you've enjoyed most about your time together today. Ask what highlights the participant experienced—those parts of the discussion that were particularly helpful to him.

• Encourage him in any ways you can from your conversation today.

• Ask him to close in prayer.

• [After the appointment, reflect on your coaching session, and fill in the following journal page to help you grow in your skills as a coach.]

~ Taking Time to Reflect on Today's COACHING Session ~

Participant's name:_____ Date:_____

During the appointment, what was happening in you while you were coaching? _____
_____
_____
_____
_____

What did you learn about yourself today as you were coaching? _____
_____
_____
_____

What did you learn from today's appointment about this participant? _____
_____
_____
_____

What would you like to do differently next time? Any prayer items? _____
_____
_____
_____

4

~ Coaching Session Four ~
Recognizing Our Spiritual Uniqueness

Outcomes:
1. To continue building a relationship of trust with the participant;
2. To discuss the participant's Spiritual Temperament Inventory and see how much she agrees or disagrees with her inventory scores;
3. To discuss the Spiritual Temperament descriptions in Chapter 3, and see how they compare with her Spiritual Temperament Inventory;
4. To introduce Chapter 4 in *WYGL?*

CONNECT
• Greet the participant and find out how the last few weeks have been.

• Follow up on the participant's Action Steps from your last meeting:
> • How did it go when you asked people how they best connected with God?
> • What insights did you gain from these conversations?
> • What did you learn about yourself this week as you paid more attention to when your own desires for God were being stirred?

• Find out what the participant thought about Chapters 2 and 3 of *WYGL?* Field any questions.

AWARENESS/ASK/LISTEN
• Discuss two of the ways people can determine their own spiritual temperaments:
> 1) First, by using the inventory in *WYGL?* (pages 21-27).
> 2) Secondly, by reading the full descriptions of the Spiritual Temperaments in Chapter 3 of *WYGL?* and identifying characteristics with which she can relate.

• Talk together about how knowing her spiritual temperament might be a valuable piece of information in her relationship with God.

• Discuss the results of the participant's Spiritual Temperament Inventory by asking:
> • After you took the Inventory, in which temperaments did you score in the High range? (page 27).

• Explain that for now, you aren't going to talk in detail about the three categories of spiritual temperament scores:
> • **High or Passionate**—those Spiritual Temperaments that are strongest and stir our passion most readily for God;
> • **Medium or Pleasurable**—those Spiritual Temperaments that we enjoy and those that nurture our love for God;
> • **Low or Potential**—those Spiritual Temperaments that are relatively unused and undeveloped. (These categories and the significance of the scores will be discussed in detail later in this Coaching Guide.)

• Because the inventory is only one way of determining the participant's most passionate spiritual preferences,[15] Ask her:
> • When you read the descriptions of the temperaments in Chapter 3 of *WYGL?*, how did your impressions compare with your Spiritual Temperament Inventory scores on page 27?

---

[15] The term "spiritual preferences" will be used interchangeably with "spiritual temperaments".

• What new perceptions did you gain from
the chapter that increased your
understanding of your own spiritual journey
and/or the journey of others?
• How does knowing your 'unique wiring'
give you more freedom to enjoy your
relationship with God?
• Have there been any changes this week in
your walk with the Lord as you've learned
more about your spiritual temperament or
'love language' with Him?

• Ask the participant what she was thinking about
Jesus as she read that He embodied *every* spiritual
temperament (He experienced His connection with
the Father during times of *silence,* showed consistent
adoration for Abba, used his *intellect* to study
Scripture, *confronted evil* and *injustice* with power and
authority, *cared* for others through a life of service,
etc).

• Ask the participant if she would like to read you
any of the prayers she wrote this week in the
Chapter 3 exercises.

ACTION
• Find out how the participant will continue
pursuing God this week. Ask:
        • How will you incorporate what you're
        learning into your walk with God?

• Are there people with whom you want to share your new insights and discoveries?

• Invite her to read Chapter 4 this week and do the exercises on pages 104, 106, 108-109.

• Write down any Action Items the participant verbalizes, and encourage her to write them down as well.

SUPPORT/HIGHLIGHTS
• In closing, share what you've enjoyed most about your time together, and find out if there have been any highlights or new discoveries for her, anything particularly helpful.

• Encourage her in any ways you can from your conversation today.

• Close in prayer.

• [After the appointment, reflect on your coaching session and fill in the following journal page to help you grow as a coach.]

~ Taking Time to Reflect on Today's COACHING Session ~

Participant's name:_____ Date:_____

During the appointment, what was happening in you while you were coaching? _____
_____
_____
_____
_____

What did you learn about yourself today as you were coaching? _____
_____
_____
_____
_____

What did you learn from today's appointment about this participant? _____
_____
_____
_____
_____

What would you like to do differently next time? Any prayer items?_____
_____
_____
_____

5

~ Coaching Session Five ~
Appreciating Spiritual Desires and Disciples

Outcomes:
1. To continue building a relationship of safety and trust with the participant;
2. To celebrate how the participant is continuing to grow in his relationship with God;
3. To discuss insights from Chapter 4 and see how the participant might be responding to God in new ways;
4. To discover how desire and discipline work together in his life;
5. To introduce Chapter 5 in *WYGL?*

CONNECT
• Greet the participant and find out how the last few weeks have been. Ask how he's doing with any of his Action Items from the last time you were together.

• Find out what the participant thought about Chapter 4 in *WYGL?* and if anything in particular was helpful or challenging.

AWARENESS/ASK/LISTEN
• Discuss how some people have asked, "Now that I know my spiritual temperament, what do I do next?" This week's lesson will address that question.

• Share how the book indicates that knowing one's spiritual temperament is an important *first step* in growing in an authentic relationship with God. Ask:
> • What did you learn from Chapter 4 about building *"the kind of partnership with God that brings a greater and more full-orbed life with Him"* (page 98)?
> • As you read this chapter, could you identify with any beneficial habits you've established over the years that have helped you preserve your spiritual life?

• Since spiritual growth requires ALL of God and ALL of us—His 100% and our 100%—ask what new behaviors or attitudes he'd like to see developed in his life in partnership with God?

• *WYGL?* emphasizes that in our relationship with Jesus, spiritual desire and discipline are interconnected. Ask:

> • What comes to mind when you hear the words, 'spiritual desire' and 'spiritual discipline'?
> • In what ways do you see your own spiritual desire and discipline playing a role in your relationship with God?

• Talk about how a discipline is simply a helpful, beneficial habit—like brushing our teeth, exercising regularly, or going to work on time, even when we don't feel like it. Some disciplines offer short-term, more immediate results (like going to bed early enough to wake up rested the next day), while other disciplines have more long-term effects that make our lives better in the future (like getting the oil changed in our cars every 3,000-5,000 miles to sustain the life of the engine). However, both short and long-term habits—both good and bad—eventually pay dividends.

• If the spiritual disciplines are indeed "love-aides"(*not ends in themselves but rather tools or vehicles that propel us toward where we want to be in our life with God*), in what areas do you want to employ some new 'tools'? (see *WYGL?* page 103).

• Adele Calhoun says, "*Transformation happens as you keep company with Jesus.... And wanting to keep company with Jesus has a staying power that 'shoulds' and 'oughts' seldom have."*[16]

> • How have you found that "keeping company with Jesus" draws you to Him in a way 'shoulds' and 'oughts' have not?
> • What fruit do you see in your life when you "keep company with Jesus"?

• *WYGL?* encourages us not to settle for a life that lacks God's fruit and strength because the Lord desires to nurture in us His beauty, grace, calmness, compassion, mercy, generosity of heart, patience, forgiveness, self-restraint, other-centered love, peace, courage, and joy. Ask the participant:

> • As you reflect on God's desire to nurture *you*, what would you like to ask Him to do in this season of your life? (You may want to share the prayer you wrote on page 109).
> • What part do *you* play in receiving the nurture God wants you to have? Be as specific as possible. (This will be discussed in more detail in Section II of *WYGL?*)

ACTION

• Who do you know whose *spiritual desire* for God inspires you, someone whose heart and spiritual passion you admire?

> • Without copying that person, what might it be like to connect with them this week and ask how they nurture the spiritual desires in their lives?

---

16 Calhoun, pages 15-16.

• Who do you know personally whose *spiritual discipline* you respect, someone whose rhythms and habits with God you highly esteem?
   • Without needing to be like them, what might happen if you connected with that person this week and asked how they nurture the spiritual disciplines in their lives?

• Find out how the participant plans to continue pursuing God this week by asking:
   • How will you incorporate what you are learning into your relationship with God?
   • How will you attend to your own spiritual desires?
   • What 'love-aides' or spiritual disciplines will you employ to see greater fruit produced in your life?
   • Are there people with whom you want to share this week what you've been learning?

• Encourage him to read Chapter 5, and do the exercises on pages 113 and 134.

• Write down any Action Items the participant verbalizes, and encourage him to write them down as well.

SUPPORT/HIGHLIGHTS

• In closing, share what you've enjoyed most about your time together, and ask if there have been any significant parts of the discussion for him?

• Encourage him in any ways you can from your conversation today.

• Invite him to close in prayer.

• [After the appointment, reflect on your coaching session and fill in the following journal page to help you grow in your skills as you progress through the coaching process.]

~ Taking Time to Reflect on Today's COACHING Session ~

Participant's name:_____ Date:_____

During the appointment, what was happening in you while you were coaching? _____

_____

_____

_____

_____

What did you learn about yourself today as you were coaching? _____

_____

_____

_____

What did you learn from today's appointment about this participant? _____

_____

_____

_____

What would you like to do differently next time? Any prayer items? _____

_____

_____

_____

6

~ Coaching Session Six ~
Celebrating the Spiritual Temperaments of Others

Outcomes:
1. To continue building a relationship of safety and trust with the participant;
2. To celebrate ways the participant is seeing her relationship with God deepen;
3. To discuss insights from Chapter 5, and how these might change the participant's relationship with others;
4. To consider how the participant might share the information she's learning about the spiritual temperaments with her family, small group, church, school, etc.;
5. To introduce Chapter 6 in *WYGL?*

CONNECT
• Greet the participant and find out how the last few weeks have been.

• How is she seeing her relationship with God and others changing?

• Follow up on her actions steps from last week, especially if she contacted someone whose spiritual desires/disciplines inspired her.

• Ask what the participant thought of Chapter 5 of *WYGL?* Field any questions.

AWARENESS/ASK/LISTEN
• Chapter Five in *WYGL?* begins with a scenario about Bruce and the small group that meets in his home. Ask the participant:
> • In your faith community, are there any ways you identify with Bruce's frustration?
> • Do you relate with any other people mentioned in the story?
> • Without disclosing names, how have you observed people worshiping in a variety of ways in your own faith-community?
> • How might your attitude change if you saw the differences as *"bold statements of how God has legitimately though diversely wired us"* rather than indicators of *"unity or disunity, maturity or immaturity, spiritual passion or spiritual indifference?"* (page 112).

66

• Discuss each statement here from *WYGL?* and decide if you agree or disagree, and why (page 114):

> • *"In the language of the spiritual temperaments, when we experience diversity in loving God under one roof, it is more than okay—it is necessary!"*

> • *"When all in the group are similar, growth may not be happening as much as when its membership comes bringing differing points of view, since change most often occurs when we are with others who think divergently, giving us an opportunity to [broaden] our own perspective."*

> • *"When we see the world through parallel—allowing differing values to emerge—then we have the best chance of operating like the body of Christ in an authentic way, united yet with our many members…. seeing more of God's nature revealed as each of us brings our small piece of God's likeness to the table."*

• What feelings do you both have as you discuss this?

• Talk about how "finding common ground" might be helpful for people in *your* faith community—in spite of differences—and discuss some ways that could happen.

> • How could you help that process?

• Converse about this statement in *WYGL?*:
*"Churches and denominations seem to cluster around
similarities in interests and spiritual temperaments"*
(page 115). If that's the case, ask the participant
which spiritual temperaments are most prevalent in
her church or denomination (put a 1 by the
temperament she thinks is most honored in her
church, then a 2 by the second most honored, and so
on):

     _____The Activist—loving God through
         confrontation with evil
     _____The Ascetic—loving God through solitude
         and simplicity
     _____The Caregiver—loving God through
         serving others
     _____The Contemplative—loving God through
         adoration
     _____The Enthusiast—loving God through
         mystery and celebration
     _____The Intellectual—loving God through the
         mind
     _____The Naturalist—loving God through
         experiencing Him out-of-doors
     _____The Sensate—loving God through the
         senses
     _____The Traditionalist—loving God through
         ritual and symbol

• In your opinion, how might putting one spiritual
temperaments above another injure the body of
Christ or even displease God?

• Ask the participant to list each of the people in her family, and 'guesstimate' each of their spiritual temperaments.
  • How might this information helpful, and how could you share with the members of your family?

• *WYGL?* explains that *teleios* is the Greek word Jesus used in Matthew 5:4 when He said: "Therefore you are to be perfect *(teleios)*, as your heavenly Father is perfect *(teleios)*". The word *teleios* means, "to bring to its finished end, to come to full maturity." It is the kind of development the Apostle Paul described in Philippians 3:12-14 when he said he had not become perfect *(teleios)*, but was, "pressing on to apprehend that for which he had been apprehended by Christ." Ask the participant:
  • What does becoming mature in Christ mean to you, and how does it effect your hunger to know Him more deeply?

• Talk about Mike Yaconelli's description of growing up spiritually when he writes:
> *"Spirituality is not a formula. It's not a test. It is a relationship—one not about competency, but about intimacy. It is not about perfection, but connection.... Spirituality is anything but a straight line; it is a mixed-up, topsy-turvy, helter skelter godliness that turns our lives into an upside down toboggan ride full of unexpected turns, surprise bumps, and*

69

*bone shattering crashes. In other words,
messy spirituality is the delirious
consequence of a life ruined by a Jesus who
will love us right into His arms."*[17]

• How do you respond to this statement?
• If you could write a one-word synonym for
"teleios," and another for *"messy spirituality"*,
what would those be?

  • *teleios:* _____

  • *messy spirituality:* _____

• How do you see *"teleios"* and *"messy
spirituality"* as necessary parts of our
authentic life with God?
• How might *"teleios"* and *"messy spirituality"*
look when they are fleshed out through our
spiritual temperaments?
• How might they look in the spiritual
temperaments of others?
• How might God be inviting that when He
says, "Come, let us reason together" (Isaiah
1:18), and "Pour out your heart to Him" (Ps.
62:8)?

---

[17] Mike Yaconelli, *Messy Spirituality* (Grand Rapids, MI: Zondervan, 2002), pages 13 and 17.

ACTION

• In light of what you're learning, what action steps will you take to grow in your *messy, teleios intimacy* with Christ this week?

•How might you assist others in growing in their *messy, teleios intimacy*, too, especially considering their spiritual temperaments?

• When it comes to nurturing compatibility and unity in your home, school, small group, and church, how might the following be helpful for you this week?
> • Understanding your own and others' wiring?
> • Sharing your discoveries and helping others better understand their own spiritual temperaments?
> • Talking openly and honestly about the various spiritual preferences in your home or church, and acknowledging—even naming—these differences, calling them what they truly are: *God Languages?*
> • Being sensitive to those whose spiritual temperaments are unlike your own—especially in your gatherings?
> • Giving yourself permission to congregate with those whose spiritual temperaments are like your own?
> • Walking and living with grace and understanding among those who are different, allowing yourself to be stretched as you learn to listen and cherish other spiritual temperaments?

• Beginning to celebrate spiritual difference wholeheartedly by developing lenses that allow you to see the world through the eyes of those who are not like you?
• Creating eclectic environments where all the spiritual temperaments are honored and find expression?

• Discuss the advantages of talking to your pastor or the leader of your organization/school/small group, etc., about fostering appreciation for different spiritual temperaments within your faith community.
• What might it be like to introduce *WYGL?* to your leaders so they can learn how God has uniquely wired each person?

• Write down the Action Items the participant verbalizes, and encourage her to write them down.

• Set a time to meet in two weeks.

SUPPORT/HIGHLIGHTS
• In closing, share what you've enjoyed most about your time together today, and ask if there have been any highlights for her, any parts of the discussion that were particularly important or helpful?

• Encourage her in any ways you can from your conversation today.

• Close in prayer.

• [After the appointment ends, reflect on your coaching session and fill in the following journal page that will help you grow in your skills as a coach.]

~ Taking Time to Reflect on Today's COACHING Session ~

Participant's name:_____ Date:_____

During the appointment, what was happening in you while you were coaching? _____
_____
_____
_____
_____

What did you learn about yourself today as you were coaching? _____
_____
_____
_____

What did you learn from today's appointment about this participant? _____
_____
_____
_____

What would you like to do differently next time? Any prayer items? _____
_____
_____
_____

7

~ Coaching Session Seven ~
Experiencing Love for God within the Spiritual Temperaments

Outcomes:
1. To continue building a relationship of safety and trust with the participant;
2. To rejoice together in how the participant is maturing in his love for God;
3. To discuss Chapter 6 and explore how the participant can experience a greater measure of God's love for him;
4. To introduce Part II of *WYGL?*

CONNECT
• Greet the participant and find out how life is going.

• How has the Lord has been meeting him this week?

• Ask how his action steps from your last meeting have been going, especially if he was able to talk to his pastor or the leader of his organization/school/small group, etc., about fostering greater awareness and appreciation of the spiritual temperaments within his faith community.

• Find out what the participant liked best about Chapter 6 of *WYGL?* Field any questions.

AWARENESS/ASK/LISTEN
• Chapter 6 in *WYGL?* is about the enormity of God's love for us, and how we can live moment-by-moment in the *overflow of the ever-flow* of God's redeeming love. Share with the participant that today's coaching session will be different in that it will be more *experiential than conversational*, and that you will be joining him in all aspects of today's 'God encounter'.

[Coaches, you may want to select two or three of the four 'experiences' in this lesson, and suggest the other(s) as action items, depending upon the time you have and the spiritual temperament of the participant.]

ACTIVITY #1—EXPERIENCING GOD'S LOVE THROUGH HIS WORD:

• It's wonderful to be nurtured in God's word and—like a sponge—just soak it in. Take turns reading these verses to one another slowly—some of which have been personalized—allowing the truth of each passage to be spoken over you.

"But now, this is what the Lord says;
He who created you, He who formed you:
'Fear not, for I have redeemed you;
I have called you by name; you are Mine.'"
(Isaiah 43:1, 7, NIV)

"In a desert land I found you,
in a barren and howling waste.
I shielded you and cared for you;
I guarded you as the apple of My eye."
(Deut 32:10, NIV)

"You are precious to Me, you are honored and I love you."
(Isaiah 43:4, NLT)

"'I will be a Father to you, and you will be my sons and
daughters,' says the Lord Almighty."
(2 Cor. 6:18, NASB)

"How precious are your thoughts about me, O God!
They are innumerable! I can't even count them;
they outnumber the grains of sand!
And when I wake up in the morning,
You are still with me!"
(Psalm 139:17-18, NLT)

*"In the same way and to the same extent that the Father
loves Me, in that same way and to that same extent I love
you. Continually bask in, remember, and drink in the full
dimension of My committed love for you."*
(John 15:9, my paraphrase)

*"You have clothed me with garments of salvation,
You have wrapped me with a robe of righteousness
as a bridegroom decks himself with a garland
and as a bride adorns herself with her jewels."*
(Isaiah 61:10, NASB

*"As the bridegroom rejoices over the bride,
so You, Lord, rejoice over me."*
(Isaiah 62:5, NASB)

*"And I saw the holy city, new Jerusalem, coming down
out of heaven from God, made ready as a bride
adorned for her husband."*
(Rev 21:2, NASB)

*"The Spirit and the bride say, 'Come!'
And let him who hears say, 'Come!'
Whoever is thirsty, let him come; and whoever wishes,
let him take the free gift of the water of life."*
(Rev 22:17, NIV)

*"Everything that touches the water of this river will live....
And wherever this water flows, everything will live."*
(Ezekiel 47:9, NLT)

• Ask the participant how it feels to be cared for like
this, drenched in God's river of liquid love?

• What is his response to God in this moment? Take
time to talk to the Lord together.

ACTIVITY #2—EXPERIENCING GOD'S LOVE THROUGH MUSIC:

• Many love songs have been written to the Lord throughout the centuries. In order to worship God through music today, sing or say the words of these songs aloud together, pausing for a few moments after each song to take in God's amazing, endless love for *you!*

Your Love Is Extravagant
by Darrell Evans
Your love is extravagant, Your friendship, intimate,
I find I'm moving to the rhythms of Your grace,
Your fragrance is intoxicating in our secret place,
Your love is extravagant.

Spread wide in the arms of Christ,
is the love that covers sin,
No greater love have I ever known,
You considered me a friend,
capture my heart again.

The Love Song of the Welsh Revival
by William Rees
Here is love, vast as the ocean,
lovingkindness as the flood,
Where the Prince of Life, our Ransom,
shed for us His precious blood.

Who His love will not remember?
Who can cease to sing His praise?
He can never be forgotten,
throughout Heav'n's eternal days.
On the mount of crucifixion,

79

fountains opened deep and wide,
Through the floodgates of God's mercy,
flowed a vast and gracious tide.

Grace and love, like mighty rivers,
poured incessant from above,
And Heav'n's peace and perfect justice,
kissed a guilty world in love.

No love is higher, no love is wider,
no love is deeper, no love is truer,
No love is higher, no love is wider,
no love is like Your love.[18]

O the Deep Deep Love of Jesus,
by Samuel Francis &Thomas Williams
O the deep, deep love of Jesus,
Vast unmeasured, boundless, free!
Rolling as a mighty ocean in its fullness over me!
Underneath me, all around me,
is the current of Thy love,
Leading onward, leading homeward,
To Thy glorious rest above!
O the deep, deep love of Jesus,
Spread His praise from shore to shore!

---

[18] Over a hundred years ago, this song became known as "The Love Song of the Revival" in Wales when a solo rang out from the small Ebenezer Baptist Church in Abertillery. A thousand people were pressed into that small church for more than four hours—leaning over the galleries and squeezing into every corner. Meetings took place night after night, with fervent prayer and passionate singing...and total disregard for the clock. In a year's time, a hundred thousand people had made a new commitment to Jesus Christ, and whole communities were being changed as men and women found themselves drawn into a powerful experience with the Lord. The sparks from this awakening ignited fires in over a dozen countries.

How He loveth, ever loveth, changeth never,
nevermore!
How He watches o'er His loved ones,
died to call them all His own;
How for them He intercedeth,
Watcheth o'er them from the throne!

O the deep, deep love of Jesus,
Love of every love the best!
'Tis an ocean full of blessing, '
Tis a haven giving rest!

O the deep, deep love of Jesus,
'Tis a heav'n of heav'ns to me;
And it lifts me up to glory,
For it lifts me up to Thee!

• Ask the participant how it feels to be immersed in
God's immeasurable ocean of love for *him?*

• What is his heart saying to God in this moment?
Take time to respond together.

ACTIVITY #3—EXPERIENCING GOD'S LOVING VOICE:

• Isn't it amazing that God—the Creator of the
universe—speaks to us, allowing us to hear His
thoughts and feelings. As implausible as that sounds,
Jesus said, *"My sheep hear My voice, and I know them,
and they follow Me"* (John 10:27).

• Invite the participant to ask the Lord to speak to
him right now to tell him what He loves about him
and the relationship you share.

• Allow Jesus to describe what He enjoys most about *you.* Listen and write what you hear Him saying:

"My child, _____ (add your name),

_____

_____

_____

_____

_____

(Write what the Lord says or brings to mind.)

• Now tell Jesus what you love most about Him, what you most enjoy in your relationship:

"Lord, in our relationship, I love You and enjoy:

_____

_____

_____

_____

_____

(Feel free to take your time to capture all you want to say to the Lord right now.)

• Ask the participant how it feels to be in this eternal, mutual love relationship with the living God—a relationship for which he was created and will spend eternity?

• What is his response to God in this moment? Take time to talk to God together.

ACTIVITY #4—REMEMBERING GOD'S ACTS OF LOVE AND MERCY:

• The Bible uses the word "remember" 170 times. God tells us to remember the *marvelous deeds* He has done for us, His people—to recall, rehearse, and retell these events to others.

• Ask the participant to think back over his life. If he were to select two pictures from his photo album of treasured moments with Jesus—times when God showed His tender love, answered prayer, brought comfort—what would those snapshots be? Ask him to take a few moments to draw those pictures below:

• [*Coach, while the participant is drawing, you can draw your own pictures from your treasured moments with Jesus; then share them later with the participant.*]

• Ask the participant how it feels to think that for all eternity, we will be with this God of endless love?

• What is his response to God in this moment? Thank and praise Jesus together.

ACTION
• Ezekiel 47 talks about a river that flows from the throne of God, and describes how we can enter this river up to our ankles, our knees, our waist… or even swim in the river and be immersed in God Himself. Ask the participant:
   • What might it look like to wade into God's river: up to your ankles, your knees, your waist… or just jump in all the way and go swimming?

• Which posture will you choose this week?
• How will you remain in the strong current of God's river of love and life the next few weeks... or longer?

• Write down the Action Items the participant verbalizes, and encourage him to write them down as well.

• Set a time to meet again in two weeks.

SUPPORT/HIGHLIGHTS
• In closing, share what you've enjoyed most about your time together today, and ask if there have been any helpful highlights for him, any parts of the discussion that were particularly important?

• Encourage him in any ways you can from your conversation today.

• Invite him to close in prayer.

• [After the appointment, reflect on your coaching session and fill in the following journal page that will help you grow in your skills through this coaching process.]

~ Taking Time to Reflect on Today's COACHING Session ~

Participant's name:_____ Date:_____

During the appointment, what was happening in you while you were coaching? _____
_____
_____
_____
_____

What did you learn about yourself today as you were coaching? _____
_____
_____
_____

What did you learn from today's appointment about this participant? _____
_____
_____
_____

What would you like to do differently next time? Any prayer items?_____
_____
_____
_____

8

~ Coaching Session Eight ~
Introducing the Spiritual Practice Exercises

Outcomes:
1. To celebrate the relationship you have shared over the last few months with the participant;
2. To discuss the participant's Spiritual Practices Inventory and see how much her preferences align with her practices;
3. To begin the Spiritual Practice Exercises in Part II of *WYGL?*
4. To encourage her to continue meeting God via all she's learned the last few months, plus utilizing the Spiritual Practice Exercises in Part II.

CONNECT
• Greet the participant and find out how she's been doing the last few weeks. Ask about her Action Items.

• How has she been enjoying the river of God's love and grace? How has the Lord been meeting her there?

• Find out what the participant liked best about Part II of *WYGL?* Discuss any questions.

• Share some of your own experiences about how God has touched your life since the two of you began meeting, and ask the participant to share her overall experience.

AWARENESS/ASK/LISTEN
• Before you look at the participant's Spiritual Practice Inventory scores on page 34 of *WYGL?*, discuss the importance of aligning our Spiritual Practices (our habits *with* God) with our Spiritual Temperaments (our preferences *for* God). Ask:
> • If you currently had unlimited time, money, and people-resources—everything you needed to know and love God more passionately—*how* you would go about developing your relationship. (Please be as specific as possible, and feel free to dream big and 'think outside the box.' Remember, in this scenario, time, money, and people-resources are of no consequence.

• Jot down what the participant says as she shares her answer.

• After she has responded, look at her chart on page 27. Discuss where she reported her own spiritual preferences to be **High**. Remind her that her preferences will fall into three categories:

> • **Her *passionate* temperaments**—those preferences that are strongest and stir her love for God most readily—where she scored *High*;
> • **Her *pleasurable* temperaments**—those preferences that she enjoys and that nurture her relationship with God—where she scored *Moderately*; and
> • **Her *potential* temperaments**—those preferences that are relatively unused and undeveloped, almost foreign to her—where she scored *Low*.

• Then have the participant look at the list of Spiritual Temperaments on page 8 of *WYGL?*

• Read the answer she gave a few moments ago back when you asked how she would pursue her relationship with God if she had unlimited resources.

> • Ask: How did your answer about your ideal pursuit of God align with your spiritual preferences as seen in your strongest Spiritual Temperament score on page 27?

• What do you learn about yourself from this?[19]

• Show the participant her Spiritual Practice Inventory results on page 34. Discuss how the author's research demonstrated the following:

> 1. The more closely someone's **spiritual preferences** *matched* their **spiritual practices** (i.e., how they were pursuing God aligned with how they liked to connect with God), the more spiritual passion they reported to have for God. In other words, when people meet God in ways they *enjoy*—even in some of those 'out of the box' venues—they felt closer to Jesus and more in love with Him.

> 2. Conversely, research showed that when spiritual preferences were *not* given expression—when people were solely doing what they were taught rather than what they enjoyed or what ignited their passion for God— their interest and satisfaction in spiritual things declined, as did their sense of closeness to God.

---

[19] Many people interviewed during the research for *WYGL?* had no idea how to draw near to God terms of their spiritual preferences. People mostly knew what had been taught or modeled for them: how to go to church, pray, read their Bibles (which are all good things). Even when all limitations were removed, people had trouble imagining new ways of communing with God. Thus, Part II of *WYGL?* was written to take individuals deeper into all nine Spiritual Temperaments so they can explore practices within their own spiritual temperaments, as well as innovative ways of connecting with God 'outside their box'.

3. Interestingly, the author found that most people did not know *how* to grow closer to God in ways that were fulfilling to them. In fact, when the question was asked, "If you had unlimited time and resources, how you would go about pursing God in a way that would increase your spiritual passion?" one person said, "Maybe I'd go to seminary." When the author reminded this person that she scored only moderately high in the Intellectual Spiritual Temperament, but quite high in the Contemplative Spiritual Temperament, the person exclaimed, "Well, that's why I've had problems all these years!"

• Just as people eat different foods, choose differing modes of exercise, and wear different clothing—primarily ones they enjoy—so our relationship with God can look differently as we can pursue Him in authentic ways that bring life to us!

• Ask the participant how the author's findings might apply to her?

• Discuss how the participant feels about beginning to work on the spiritual practices in Part II of *WYGL?*—exercises designed to help her develop her intimacy with God in deeper, broader, and more meaningful ways.

• Remind her that while it may take awhile to feel the benefits of these exercises, she can be assured that her relationship with God *will* grow if she is seeking Him authentically with all her heart. Hebrews 11:6 says: *"And without faith it is impossible to please God, because anyone who comes to Him must believe that He exists and that He rewards those who earnestly seek Him."*
> •When we seek God, *He* becomes our Reward: He gives us His presence, power, peace, pardon, provision, and perspective.

• Discuss what the participant thinks about this statement in *WYGL?*: *"The goal of the spiritual exercises is to know and love God more fully and deeply, and because He is our spiritual Coach, Companion, and Cheerleader, we can expect Him to meet us each time we show up [for practice]!"* (pg 160).
> • In what ways have you seen God *coach* and *cheer you on* as you've met Him over the years, especially the last few months?
> •How are you, by faith, expecting God to meet you in the months to come as you seek Him?

ACTION
• Have the participant find her highest Spiritual Temperament score, and begin the exercises for that Spiritual Temperament in Part II this week.

• After she completes the exercises for her highest Spiritual Temperament, invite her to begin the exercises for the other temperaments in her High range; then do the exercises for the temperaments in her Medium range, and so on until she has completed the exercises for all nine temperaments, increasing her capacity to connect with God—every day in every way.[20]

• Discuss her plans to consistently remain in her current rhythm with the Lord, the goal being to create a genuine connection with Jesus and access His transforming grace.

• Talk about this statement by Richard Foster called, "Invited Grace":

> "God will not enter many areas of our life uninvited.
> So we invite God to enter every experience of life:
> We invite God to set our spirit free for worship and adoration.
> We invite God to animate our preaching and praying and singing.
> We invite God to heal our bodies.
> We invite God to inform our minds with creative ideas for our business enterprises.
> We invite God to touch broken relationships and resolve conflicts at work or home.
> We invite God to make our homes holy places of worship and study and work and play and lovemaking.
> We invite . . . we invite. Perhaps we could speak of this as 'invited grace.'"

---

[20] Though our preferences don't usually change, the research for *WYGL?* showed that the *broader* the spiritual practice scores across all nine spiritual temperaments, the more *hungry* people reported to be for God. In other words, the more experience people had in connecting with God in a variety of ways, the stronger their desire for Him seemed to be. Thus, learning to meet God through a range of spiritual practice exercises is likely to result in greater passion for Him.

• Discuss any areas in your lives where you want and need more of God's 'Invited Grace'?

• Think through some 'next steps' together— possibilities that are available for the participant now that the eight coaching sessions are coming to an end.

• If the time you've spent together has been meaningful to both of you, and if a true spiritual friendship has been established, you may want to continue meeting together as you go through the spiritual practice exercises in Part II of *WYGL?*

• Set a time to meet for lunch or coffee in the next few months to see how you're both doing, or plan a special event to commemorate the culmination of your commitment to completing *WYGL?* Consider allowing this to be an opportunity to share your journey by inviting your family or faith community to come hear how you've grown—making Jesus the center of your life—describing for them how your new awareness of your Spiritual Temperaments and Spiritual Practices have augmented your life.

SUPPORT/HIGHLIGHTS
• In closing, share what you've gained from these eight sessions together, and highlight the changes you've seen in one another over the months. Make this final time both a celebration of God's faithfulness to you—and yours to Him—as you affirm one another.

• Encourage her in any ways you can from your conversation today.

• Both close in prayer.

• [After the appointment, reflect on your coaching session and fill in the following journal page that will help you grow in your skills through this coaching process.]

~ Taking Time to Reflect on Today's COACHING Session ~

Participant's name:_____ Date:_____

During the appointment, what was happening in you while you were coaching? _____
_____
_____
_____
_____

What did you learn about yourself today as you were coaching? _____
_____
_____
_____
_____

What did you learn from today's appointment about this participant? _____
_____
_____
_____
_____

What would you like to do differently next time? Any prayer items?_____
_____
_____
_____

A SPIRITUAL FORMATION FRAMEWORK

Coaching Around a Biblical Model of Spiritual Formation

Because this Coaching Guide is designed to assist believers in their spiritual journey—seeing their whole lives transformed by Jesus (2 Cor. 3:18, Gal 4:19)—it's important to discuss the overall process of spiritual formation, and what it means to be formed into the image of Christ.

Let's begin with a definition:

> Christian Spiritual Formation is that which takes place in the believer's life as God's Spirit transforms us through our ever-deepening intimacy with the Trinity. Changed from the inside out through our love relationship with Christ, our inner life with God and outer life with others becomes one in which Christ's reflection is seen *in and through us*, impacting

the total life and character of the believer—
encompassing our whole-life response to the
Triune God.[21]

Through the years, many people have offered
descriptions of how this transformation occurs
and becomes visible in the believer's life, such as:

> "[Spiritual formation] is simply the
> increasing influence, vitality, and sway of
> God's Spirit in us... the magnificent
> choreography of the Holy Spirit within the
> human spirit moving us toward communion
> with both Creator and creation. The spiritual
> life is thus grounded in relationship. It has to
> do with God's way of relating to us and our
> way of relating to God."[22]

> "It is the interior freedom [that] allows us to
> be completely given over in love to God and
> others at any given moment.... the ability to
> live from an inner security that frees us from
> self-interest, self-consciousness, and self-
> protection in utter responsiveness to the
> Spirit of God within and among us....

> Then we're not limited to or driven by the
> expectations of others, but can fully embrace

---

[21] This definition was adapted from Imago Christi, a covenant
community within Church Resource Ministries. For more information,
see: www.imagochristi.org.

[22] Marjorie Thompson, *Soul Feast: An Invitation to the Christian Spiritual
Life* (Westminster John Knox Press, Reprinted in 2005).

what is most authentic within us and offer it
freely to the world."[23]

"[It] is enforcing Christ's victory over Satan....
and implementing upon earth heaven's
decisions concerning the affairs of men."[24]

Jesus also describes this process when He says:
"The goal is for them to be one—just as You and
I are one, Father; may they be one heart and
mind with Us.... I gave them the same glory You
gave Me so they'd be one as We are one—I in
them and You in Me. And their oneness will be
mature, and show that You love them just as
much as You love Me" (John 17:21-23, The
Message). [Note: God the Father loving us *as
much* as He loves God the Son: now *that's*
transformative!]

In John 17, the Greek word for *mature* is *teleios*, which
this guide has already defined as: *brining to an end,
making complete, reaching its goal, maturing*. In other
words, as we develop, we come to:
  • know the Father *just as the Son knows the Father,*
  • trust the Father *just as the Son trusts the Father,*
  • love the Father *just as the Son loves the Father,*

[23] Ruth Haley Barton and Lynne Hybels, *Longing for More: A Woman's
Path to Transformation in Christ* (IVP Books, 2007).

[24] Paul Billheimer, *Destined For the Throne* (Christian Literature Crusade,
1975).

- do the works of the Father *just as the Son does them*...bringing us to maturity and "all the fullness of God" (Eph 3:19).

The Apostle Paul said this maturity is visible when believers are able to move "rhythmically and easily with each other, efficient and graceful in response to God's Son, [as] fully mature adults, fully developed within and without, fully alive like Christ... [then we are] grown up" (Eph 4:13, *The Message*). This process happens only as we are deeply imbedded in God Himself in an all-consuming, sacred-life journey "so all-inclusive that even the smallest child may come.... Every other journey and every other ambition pale in comparison. This one challenge adds meaning and definition to all of life's other pursuits. Those who respond to the invitation find little else to live for. Those who say no spend their lives looking for an adequate replacement. And there is none to be found—anywhere."[25]

Although this journey of being spiritually formed is not altogether linear in its development, scripture tells us this growth is *ongoing* (2 Peter 3:18; 2 Corinthians 4:16; Col 1:9); *transformative* (Col 3: 10; Roman 12:2; 2 Corinthians 3:18); and *progressive*.

One of the most basic descriptions in God's word of becoming a mature believer is found in the apostle

---

[25] Bill Johnson, *Face to Face with God* (Charisma House, 2007).

John's first epistle.[26] Let's take a look at each of the three stages mentioned in 1 John 2:12-14:

> *"I am writing to you, little children, because your sins have been forgiven you for His name's sake. I am writing to you, fathers, because you know Him who has been from the beginning. I am writing to you, young men, because you have overcome the evil one. I have written to you, children, because you know the Father. I have written to you, fathers, because you know Him who has been from the beginning. I have written to you, young men, because you are strong, and the word of God abides in you, and you have overcome the evil one"*
> *(1John 2:12-14).*

1. Little Children: When we first come to Christ, we are brought into God's family as "little children" with our faith developing as we come to understand what it means to live and walk in the Lord's love and grace. In this phase of the journey, we grow in our awareness of being completely accepted in the Beloved, having all our sins forgiven, and understanding in the simplest form what it means to be adopted into God's own family—complete with an eternal inheritance. This phase is characterized by and may include:

---

[26] Many books have written detailing our spiritual development, such as Janet Hagberg and Robert Guelich, *The Critical Journey: Stages in the Life of Faith* (Sheffield Publishers, 2008); Teresa of Avila and E. Peers, *The Interior Castle* (Wilder Publications, 2008); R. Thomas Ashbrook, *Mansions of the Heart: Exploring the Seven Stages of Spiritual Growth* (Jossey-Bates, 2009).

- personal discipleship;
- learning how to authentically connect with Jesus;
- beginning to utilize the spiritual disciplines (especially prayer and Bible Study);
- becoming knit into the body of Christ with other believers;
- receiving deliverance prayer;
- knowing God as Father and ourselves as His beloved child.

Important issues and coaching questions for this phase of development:[27]

A. How is the realization that I am God's child increasing, and how am I seeing that translated into my daily interactions?

B. In what ways am I recognizing God's presence and goodness in my life?

C. When in the midst of internal and external struggles, how real is my awareness of God's grace, and how am I walking each day in the Lord's peace—experiencing His forgiveness even when I know I don't deserve it?

---

[27] These questions were developed from studying 1John 2:12-14, as well as from observing the stages in Teresa of Avila's *Interior Castle*, and Tom Ashbrook's *Mansions of the Heart*. Special thanks to Bill O'Byrne and all my friends in Imago Christi, and to Ardath Smith, Dr. Steve Hoke, and Dr. Jeremy Stefano for their assistance in reviewing some of these questions.

D. How is my understanding of God's trust-worthiness solidifying, and how well am I able to differentiate the attributes of my Heavenly Father from those of others, especially my earthly father?

E. In what ways am I learning to truly be *with* God?

F. How am I developing a life-style of discipleship, including a growing desire to please and honor God?

G. How am I learning to engage God through His word and prayer?

H. How am I experiencing my identity as a child of the King, seeing myself more from who God's word says than I am what my past says about me?

I. How have I grown in knowing myself and how my unique 'spiritual wiring' helps me connect authentically with God? In what ways am I utilizing meaningful spiritual practices to grow in that life-giving connection?

J. How is my daily relationship with God becoming characterized by His love, joy, peace, truth, and grace versus a posture of obeying Christian rules—minding the shoulds and should not's, avoiding guilt, doing good *for* love rather than *from* love, or being prompted by a fear of being judged by self and others?

K. How is the community of faith impacting my outlook on life, my relationship with God, and my attitudes toward others and myself?

L. How am I aligning myself with more mature brothers and sisters in the faith, asking them to teach and mentor me and speak truth into my life?

2. Young Men and Women: During this developmental stage, believers are gaining strength and maturity as they learn to walk consistently in God's word and the power of His Spirit. God's truth is now becoming firmly internalized, spiritual warfare is more clearly understood, discernment is increasing, and greater joy and spiritual victory typifies one's relationship with the Father, Son, and Spirit. This phase may be characterized by and include:

- an ongoing and ever deepening knowledge of the Bible;
- an ongoing surrender of every aspect of life to the Lordship of Christ;
- the ability to operate in the spiritual battle long-term while keeping God's perspective;

- knowing how to use one's spiritual authority to bring God's Kingdom to earth;
- having received and now beginning to minister healing prayer;
- having a spiritual mentor, coach, or companion;
- and knowing Christ as friend and ourselves as friends of God.

Important issues and coaching questions for this phase of development:

A. How am I growing in my understanding of God's Spirit and the invisible kingdom realities?

B. Though I may have known Jesus for a long time, how is my intimacy with Him increasing—apart from trying to just manage sin or improve my behavior?

C. How am I dealing with the more subtle temptations within, such as pride, jealously, and envy, and as God discloses my motivations at deeper levels, how am I internalizing His grace?

D. How am I learning to balance opportunities to serve God with time spent enjoying Him?

E. In what ways are my heart-motivations becoming more about love for God than duty?

F. How am I managing to live by faith during prolonged seasons of spiritual dryness?

G. What does pursing freedom from habitual sin look like in my life—even in areas I've submitted to God but haven't been able to master—so that I can love Him and others more fully?

H. How am I walking daily in my identity as a co-heir and partner with God, seeing myself consistently as God sees me rather than believing what my feelings or others say about me?

I. How am I gaining a more holistic awareness of spiritual warfare without giving the enemy unnecessary attention?

J. Where am I finding a spiritual coach or director to accompany me on this journey and speak into my life?

K. Who is ministering inner healing prayer to me so I can address any blockages or walls within?

L. How am I learning to pray and minister with greater spiritual authority?

M. Where am I receiving training to minister physical healing, deliverance prayer, inner healing?

N. How am I learning to accompany others in their spiritual journey?

4.   **Fathers and Mothers in the Faith:** As fathers and mothers who know *(ginosko)* and experience a deep, abiding love relationship with God, that connection has now become the essence and fruit of one's life—through seasons of trial or elation, desolation or consolation, fruitfulness or walking solely by faith. God's Spirit and one's intimacy with the Godhead define who we are, and Christ-like character and proven maturity *(teleios)* have become our habit. This phase may be characterized by:
  • walking steadily in the certainty of God's goodness and presence;
  • knowing God more deeply as He reveals Himself in mystery;
  • demonstrating wisdom, joy, and love for others as an ongoing lifestyle;
  • continuing to walk in our delegated authority to bring God's Kingdom to earth wherever we go;
  • companioning others as they grow in the Lord and speaking into their lives;

107

• knowing Jesus as Bridegroom and ourselves as His cherished Bride.

Important issues and coaching questions for this phase of development:

A. How am I attending to my deep longing for intimacy with the triune God, i.e., how am I making time and space to respond to God's invitation of love?

B. Where am I finding a group of people with whom I can fellowship who are serious about the contemplative life, listening prayer, and deepening their intimacy with Jesus—a safe place to explore my spiritual longings with others?

C. In what ways have I been "seeing" and "feeling" God in prayer and all of life, knowing and loving God for God's sake?

D. How has my *doing* and *being* merged, causing everything in my life to be an act of worship as I transition from serving to loving, responding more deeply to God's presence, following His lead every moment of my life?

E. How have I tasted the divine romance and a deeper awareness of God's transforming power?

F. How has my experience in prayer changed, becoming more intuitive and responsive as God leads my surrendered heart?

G. In what ways am I becoming familiar with supernatural experiences, seeing my growth coming more from God's initiative than my own?

H. How is God's compassion for the poor and those He loves breaking my heart as I live in union with Him?

I. How have I maintained a rhythm of getting away to be still and listen to the Lord as He leads—perhaps in a spiritual retreat setting?

J. How am I growing through becoming a spiritual director, spiritual companion, or spiritual friend to others, allowing them to speak into my life as I speak into theirs?

K. How is my time with God becoming more of a place where He sets the agenda and takes me into greater mystery?

L. As my hunger for God intensifies, how am I dealing with the heightened sense of my own sin, allowing it to become a springboard into God's presence and holiness?

M. As I experience God in mystery, how am I tolerating feelings of uncertainty, lack of control, and the inner awareness that I no longer have all the answers?

N. How am I yearning to be healed so that I can more freely give and receive love to God and others?

O. In what ways am I participating in the life of the church based on what I can give, rather than what I can receive?

P. How is my relationship with God more about the two of us "being in love" as I attend to Him?

Q. How am I experiencing the Sacred Marriage, Holy Union, or my Betrothal to Jesus, becoming unaware of the distinction between God and myself?

R. In what ways have all attachments to things created declined so that my aim in life has become solely God and other focused, seeing the love of God and neighbor reliably placed above my own life?

ABOUT THE AUTHOR

Since 1996, Dr. Myra Perrine has served with Church Resource Ministries, an interdenominational missions agency dedicated to leadership development for the Church worldwide. She is a also a spiritual director and LIFE Coach, as well as an adjunct professor at Simpson University and Tozer Theological Seminary. With a background in education, she has done ministry in more than 40 nations, always bringing a combination of grace, truth, laughter, & freedom wherever she goes. Her passion to know her Lord and lead others into greater intimacy with Him has produced such books as: *What's Your God Language? Connecting with God Through Your Unique Spiritual Temperament (Tyndale, 2007), Touching the Hem of His Garment: A Guide for Encountering God, Basking in the Warmth of God's Love, Hearing the Voice of the Shepherd,* and *Passionate Spirituality: Preparing for the Bridegroom.* She and her husband, Dan, live in Redding, California, where Dan directs Advancing Leaders International, a ministry that develops Christian leaders in third world countries through education and coaching (http://www.advancingleaders.org).

CPSIA information can be obtained at www.ICGtesting.com
Printed in the USA
LVOW121745200412

278511LV00024B/38/P